CATS
SET III

Bombay Cats

Julie Murray
ABDO Publishing Company

visit us at
www.abdopub.com

Published by ABDO Publishing Company, 4940 Viking Drive, Edina, Minnesota 55435.
Copyright © 2003 by Abdo Consulting Group, Inc. International copyrights reserved in
all countries. No part of this book may be reproduced in any form without written
permission from the publisher.

Printed in the United States.

Photo Credits: Corbis pp. 5, 7, 9, 15, 17, 19, 21; Animals Animals pp. 11, 13
Contributing Editors: Tamara L. Britton, Kristin Van Cleaf, Stephanie Hedlund
Book Design & Graphics: Neil Klinepier

Library of Congress Cataloging-in-Publication Data

Murray, Julie, 1969-
    Bombay cats / Julie Murray.
      p. cm. -- (Cats. Set III)
    Summary: An introduction to the origins, physical characteristics, and behavior of the
Bombay cat, with information on the choosing and care of a Bombay kitten.
    Includes bibliographical references (p.).
    ISBN 1-57765-862-0
      1. Bombay cat--Juvenile literature. [1. Bombay cat. 2. Cats.] I. Title.

SF449.B65 M87 2002
636.8'22--dc21
                                                        2001056727

Contents

Lions, Tigers, and Cats

The first cats lived about 35 million years ago. There are several different types of cats. But they all belong to the animal family **Felidae**. There are 38 different species in this family.

Cats are organized into three different categories. Examples of big cats are lions, tigers, jaguars, and leopards. The small cats include **domestic** cats, lynx, and bobcats. Cheetahs are in a group by themselves.

Domestic cats are believed to be the ancestors of the African wildcat. They were tamed about 4,000 years ago in Egypt. Today, there are more than 40 different recognized **breeds** of domestic cats.

The bobcat is in the small cat group, just like the Bombay!

Bombay Cats

Nikki Horner of Kentucky created Bombays in 1958. She wanted miniature black panthers with copper eyes. So Horner crossed a black American Shorthair and a sable Burmese to create this **breed**.

Bombay cats resemble the black leopard of India. So they were named after the city of Bombay, India. They are recognized for their shiny, **patent leather**-like coats.

Bombay cats are very intelligent. And they are great to play with. Bombays can be taught many tricks, including how to fetch and walk on a leash.

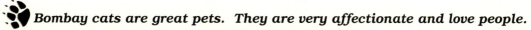

Bombay cats are great pets. They are very affectionate and love people.

Qualities

Bombays are ideal family pets. They get along well with children and other pets. They are affectionate cats who love attention. Bombays will even lie across a paper you are reading to get you to notice them.

Bombay cats do not like to be left alone. They desire company. If Bombays are going to be left alone, they prefer another cat to play with.

Bombay cats are fairly quiet. They have a soft but distinctive voice. They are playful cats without being **hyperactive**. Bombay cats are intelligent, **confident**, and friendly.

Coat and Color

Bombay cats have a shiny, jet-black coat. It is short, close lying, and satiny. Black is the only recognized color for the **breed**. Some Bombays have sable-colored coats. But these cats cannot compete in cat shows.

Bombay kittens are born a light brown color. Their coats darken and become sleeker with age. It may take up to two years for kittens to achieve their full color. Adult Bombays' fur should be black all the way to the roots.

Like all kittens, Bombays' eyes are blue at birth. They slowly turn a shade of copper or gold. For cat shows, copper is the more desired eye color. The bright shade stands out against the breed's black fur. Bombays also have a black nose and black paw pads.

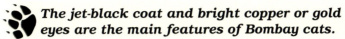
The jet-black coat and bright copper or gold eyes are the main features of Bombay cats.

Size

Bombays are medium-sized cats. Their bodies are strong, firm, and muscular. Surprisingly, they can weigh between 6 and 11 pounds (3 and 5 kg). Male Bombays are often larger than females.

Bombay cats have a round head with a short to medium-sized **muzzle**. Their ears are wide at the base and rounded at the tips. Bombays' eyes are big, round, and widely spaced across their face.

Bombay cats have a straight, medium-length tail. It tapers toward the tip. They keep their round paws well groomed.

Bombay cats are heavier than they look. Some cats can weigh 11 pounds (5 kg)! Bombays need a balanced diet to keep them from becoming overweight.

Care

All cats keep themselves clean. They do this by licking their fur often. Bombays only need to be rubbed occasionally to maintain their glossy coat. This can be done by stroking them with your hand. Or you can rub their coat with a **chamois** about once a week.

Like all cats, Bombays will frequently need to sharpen their claws. This is a natural behavior for cats. Providing them with a scratching post will save your furniture from damage.

All cats love to play and Bombays are no different. Movement is important for their enjoyment. So try to provide them with toys that they can move. A ball, **catnip** mouse, or anything they can move with their paws will be good.

It is a natural instinct for cats to bury their waste. So they should be trained to use a **litter box**. The litter box needs to be cleaned every day. Cats should also be **spayed** or **neutered** unless you are planning on **breeding** them.

Bombays keep themselves well groomed. But rubbing them with your hand will also remove loose fur.

Feeding

All cats are **carnivores**. They require food that is high in protein, such as meat or fish. Cats can be very picky and do not like changes in their diet.

Homemade diets usually do not provide the **nutrients** that cats need. A better choice is commercial cat food. It comes in three types. They are dry, semidry, and canned. Each offers similar nutritional value.

Dry foods are the most convenient. They can prevent **tartar** buildup on your cat's teeth. Canned foods are the most appealing to cats. But they do not stay fresh for very long.

Cats also need fresh water every day. Your cat may love to drink milk. But many cats are unable to **digest** milk. It will often make them sick. Cats also love treats. You can find a variety of treats at your local pet store.

Milk isn't good for most cats. These cats are getting a rare treat!

Kittens

Baby cats are called kittens. Cats are **pregnant** for about 65 days before the kittens are born. Bombays have about four kittens per **litter**.

All kittens are born blind and helpless. They need to drink their mother's milk for the first three weeks. Then they start to eat solid food. Most kittens stop drinking their mother's milk when they are about eight weeks old.

Kittens start becoming independent when they are about three weeks old. By then they can see, hear, and stand on their own. At about seven weeks, they can run and play. When kittens are 12 weeks old, they can be sold or given away.

 Most kittens are curious about the things around them. They begin exploring and playing when they are about seven weeks old.

Buying a Kitten

A healthy cat will live about 14 to 16 years. A kitten becomes very attached to its owner. So before you buy a kitten, be sure you will be able to take care of it for as long as it lives.

There are many places to get a kitten. A qualified **breeder** is the best place to buy a **purebred** kitten. When buying from a breeder, be sure to get the kitten's **pedigree** papers and health records. Pet shelters, veterinarians, and cat shows are also good places to find a kitten.

When choosing a kitten, check to see that it is healthy. Its ears, nose, mouth, and fur should all be clean. Its eyes should be bright and clear. The kitten should be alert and playful in its surroundings.

Choosing a kitten that is right for you is very important! Be careful to get a kitten that is healthy and active.

Glossary

breed - a group of cats that shares the same appearance and characteristics. A breeder is a person who raises cats. Raising cats is often called breeding them.

carnivore - an animal or plant that eats meat.

catnip - the dried leaves and stems of a plant in the mint family. Catnip is used as a stuffing in cat toys because some cats are attracted to its strong smell.

chamois - a soft, pliable leather or cloth.

confident - sure of one's self.

digest - to break down food in the stomach.

domestic - animals that are tame.

Felidae - the Latin name for the cat family.

hyperactive - more active than usual or desirable.

litter - all of the kittens born at one time to a mother cat.

litter box - a box where cats dispose of their waste.

muzzle - an animal's nose and jaws.

neuter - to remove a male animal's reproductive organs.

nutrients - vitamins and minerals that all living things need to survive.

patent leather - a leather with a smooth, glossy surface.

pedigree - a record of an animal's ancestors.

pregnant - having one or more babies growing within the body.

purebred - an animal whose parents are both from the same breed.

spay - to remove a female animal's reproductive organs.

tartar - a crust that forms on the teeth. Tartar is made of saliva, food particles, and salts.

Web Sites

Would you like to learn more about Bombays? Please visit **www.abdopub.com** to find up-to-date Web site links to more information on the Bombay breed. These links are routinely monitored and updated to provide the most current information available.

Index